FROM THE EARTH
How Resources Are Made

HOW COAL IS FORMED

BY BLAIR BELTON

Gareth Stevens
PUBLISHING

Please visit our website, www.garethstevens.com. For a free color catalog of all our high-quality books, call toll free 1-800-542-2595 or fax 1-877-542-2596.

Library of Congress Cataloging-in-Publication Data

Names: Belton, Blair, author.
Title: How coal is formed / Blair Belton.
Description: New York : Gareth Stevens Publishing, [2017] | Series: From the
  earth: how resources are made | Includes bibliographical references and
  index.
Identifiers: LCCN 2016000747 | ISBN 9781482447033 (pbk.) | ISBN 9781482447071 (library bound) | ISBN
9781482447064 (6 pack)
Subjects: LCSH: Coal–Juvenile literature. | Carbon cycle
  (Biogeochemistry)–Juvenile literature. | Coal mines and mining–Juvenile
  literature.
Classification: LCC TP325 .B448 2017 | DDC 553.2/4–dc23
LC record available at http://lccn.loc.gov/2016000747

Published in 2017 by
Gareth Stevens Publishing
111 East 14th Street, Suite 349
New York, NY 10003

Copyright © 2017 Gareth Stevens Publishing

Designer: Laura Bowen
Editor: Therese Shea

Photo credits: Cover, pp. 1–32 (title bar) Dimec/Shutterstock.com; cover, pp. 1–32 (text box) mattasbestos/
Shutterstock.com; cover, pp. 1–32 (background) Alina G/Shutterstock.com; cover, p. 1 (coal) voronas/
Shutterstock.com; p. 5 (top) Andreas Einsiedel/Dorling Kindersley/Getty Images; p. 5 (bottom) Coprid/
Shutterstock.com; p. 7 Dave King/Dorling Kindersley/Getty Images; p. 9 Karen Grigoryan/Shutterstock.com;
p. 11 (top) courtesy of NASA.com; p. 11 (bottom) Grisha Bruev/Shutterstock.com; p. 13 Alain Le Garsmeur/
Hulton Archive/Getty Images; p. 15 (top) Dorling Kindersley/Getty Images; p. 15 (bottom) Lee Prince/
Shutterstock.com; p. 16 Print Collector/Hulton Archive/Getty Images; p. 17 (lignite) Jan Gottwald/Shutterstock.com;
p. 17 (bituminous) www.sandatlas.org/Shutterstock.com; p. 17 (anthracite) Gary Ombler/Dorling Kindersley/
Getty Images; p. 19 De Agostini Picture Library/Getty Images; p. 21 Jim Parkin/Shutterstock.com; p. 23 Kbh3rd/
Wikimedia Commons; p. 24 imantsu/Shutterstock.com; p. 25 Nenad Zivkovic/Shutterstock.com; p. 27 (solar panels)
Smileus/Shutterstock.com; p. 27 (wind turbines) pedrosala/Shutterstock.com; p. 27 (geothermal) Designua/
Shutterstock.com; p. 29 Kevin Frayer/Getty Images AsiaPac/Getty Images.

Printed in the United States of America

CPSIA compliance information: Batch #CS16GS: For further information contact Gareth Stevens, New York, New York at 1-800-542-2595.

CONTENTS

Words in the glossary appear in **bold** type the first time they are used in the text.

FROM ANCIENT PLANTS

Coal is a type of rock made from plants. Most coal comes from plants that lived before the dinosaurs did!

People have used coal as a source of energy for hundreds of years. Today, it's used in a process that produces electricity. The coal is burned to heat water, which makes steam, which in turn drives the moving parts of **generators**. Over 40 percent of the electricity in the world is made by burning coal. In the United States, 93 percent of the coal burned is used to generate electric power. Most remaining coal is used in the iron, concrete, and paper industries.

CHARCOAL ISN'T COAL!

You may have seen charcoal on a grill. It's not the same as coal. Charcoal is made by partially burning wood (and sometimes animal matter) and pressing it into pieces. Charcoal is used on grills because it burns steady and hot and produces less smoke than wood. Charcoal is made by people, while coal is made by nature over millions of years.

Coal is a fossil fuel, or a fuel that comes from the remains of prehistoric plants or animals. This photo shows the different stages of coal formation beginning with plants.

vegetation

peat

brown coal

household coal

highest-quality coal

charcoal (man-made)

THE AMAZING CARBON ATOM

Coal is mostly made of the element carbon. Each carbon atom is able to bind, or hold on to, four other atoms. Since carbon can bind in so many ways, pure carbon appears in different forms, such as diamonds or graphite. (Graphite is the black part inside a pencil.)

Carbon atoms can also bind with other types of atoms to form **molecules**. Coal is made from large molecules that contain carbon and other elements. Carbon burns, while other elements in coal either don't burn and remain as leftover ash or escape as part of the coal's smoke.

FOOD IS MADE FROM CARBON

The "carbo" in carbohydrates stands for "carbon." Photosynthesis is a process in which plants (and some other organisms) use sunlight, water, and the gas carbon dioxide to make sugar, oxygen, and later starch. Sugar and starch are carbohydrates. When plants are made into food such as pasta, we eat these carbohydrates (and carbon!).

coal

Carbon takes many forms. This photo shows the carbon compounds coal and charcoal and pure carbon as graphite and diamonds. The pencil provides a comparison for size.

charcoal

graphite

diamonds

pencil

7

WHERE DID CARBON COME FROM?

When Earth formed about 4.5 billion years ago, carbon was one element that made up the planet. It was trapped underground. **Volcanoes** freed carbon as well as other elements and gases into Earth's atmosphere. Perhaps as much as 200 times more carbon dioxide made up that early atmosphere than exists in today's atmosphere!

Organisms called cyanobacteria in the early oceans took in some of the carbon dioxide, using it for photosynthesis. The process also released, or let free, oxygen into the atmosphere. Slowly, over hundreds of millions of years, the atmosphere changed into the atmosphere of today that can support animal life. Carbon is a basis for all life on Earth.

A LITTLE CARBON GOES A LONG WAY

Today, in every 10,000 molecules of air, just 3 or 4 molecules are carbon dioxide. Plants collect these carbon dioxide molecules during photosynthesis to make food and grow leaves, stems, and seeds. Plants are almost one-half carbon. In fact, carbon is found in all living things, including people!

Scientists think the mostly carbon dioxide atmospheres of Mars and Venus are somewhat like Earth's early atmosphere.

THE CARBON CYCLE

The process of carbon moving between living things and the **environment** is called the carbon cycle. You've read that plants contain carbon. Animals eat plants for food and take in their carbon. When both plants and animals die, the carbon they contain is released back into the cycle as their bodies break down. Carbon is also released when animals breathe out carbon dioxide.

The carbon cycle isn't always a fast process. Sometimes plants fall into swamps or **bogs** where they don't rot because of the lack of oxygen. They may then be covered by sediment—bits of sand, rock, and stone—trapping the carbon in the earth.

BURIED TREASURE

Over millions of years, a swamp or bog can disappear. How does this happen? It may be completely buried by sediment or dry up as the climate in an area changes. The carbon in a swamp or bog can then be trapped for millions more years, slowing the carbon cycle.

This illustration of the carbon cycle shows how carbon travels around Earth.

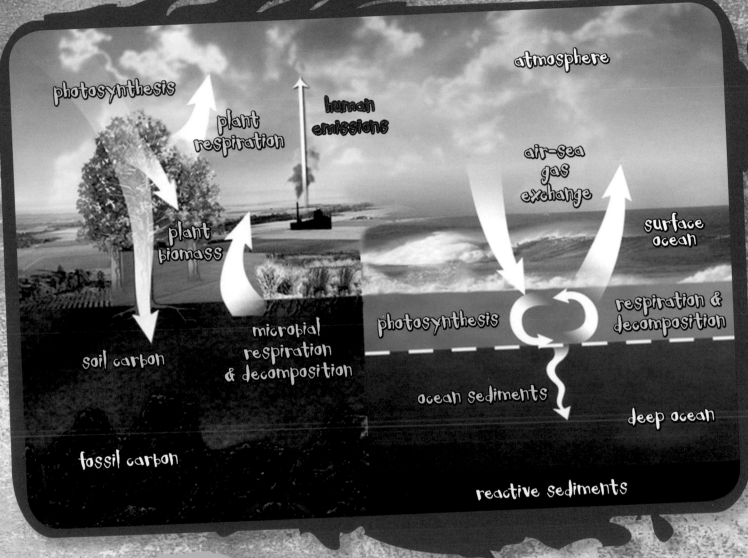

photosynthesis

plant respiration

human emissions

atmosphere

air-sea gas exchange

surface ocean

plant biomass

photosynthesis

respiration & decomposition

microbial respiration & decomposition

soil carbon

ocean sediments

deep ocean

fossil carbon

reactive sediments

bog

PEAT: THE FIRST STEP

Over hundreds or even thousands of years, preserved or partially decomposed, or broken down, plants can pile up in thick, wet layers known as peat. Peat often forms in large **depressions** that are full of water. Without oxygen, the plant matter doesn't break down quickly. Peat is the first step in coal formation.

When peat is covered by sediment, the weight of the sediment squeezes it. This force presses out the water and forces carbon molecules to bind together. Over millions of years, sediment layers atop peat apply more and more pressure as well as heat. Under these conditions, coal can form.

PEAT FOR FUEL

Even though peat doesn't contain as much carbon as coal, people still use it as fuel to heat their homes. The peat is dug up in cubes from the ground. It's soft enough to be cut with a knife. It's then dried out. After drying, the peat can be burned in a fireplace.

A man cuts pieces of peat from a bog. The Bog of Allen in Ireland and the Dismal Swamp in Virginia are two large peat bogs. Peat bogs may be from 5 to 30 feet (1.5 to 9 m) deep.

13

FROM PEAT TO COAL

Pressure and heat can transform, or change, peat into a form of coal called lignite over time. Lignite is sometimes called brown coal. It's usually yellow to dark brown. Lignite is harder than peat, but still crumbles. If left millions of more years, heat and pressure squeeze the lignite into subbituminous coal. It's darker and harder than lignite.

After more time, heat, and pressure, subbituminous coal turns into bituminous coal, which is dark brown or black. This is the most abundant, or plentiful, type of coal. Under yet more heat and pressure, anthracite is formed over time. Anthracite is the rarest type of coal.

COKING COAL

Bituminous coal, with its abundance, low water content, and high **heat value**, has the most uses among the coals, including steam generation in electric power plants. Bituminous coal is also coked, or heated to make it nearly pure carbon. It's then used to remove the impurities of metal, a process called refining.

14

Conditions must be perfect for coal formation. There must be enough plant matter and enough moisture, or wetness, to keep it from rotting. Many coal **deposits** formed where depressions were subsiding, or sinking, allowing more moisture and plants to fill them.

15

Coal is ranked according to the amount of change it has undergone from peat to anthracite. These changes affect coal's physical and chemical properties. Low-rank coals are low in carbon, but high in hydrogen and oxygen content. They have the most moisture. High-rank coals are high in carbon, but low in hydrogen and oxygen.

Coal that contains more carbon produces more heat when burned. Anthracite is the highest rank of all the coals. It has the most carbon and produces the most heat and least smoke. However, it's the rarest coal, so it's not used as often.

a gasworks in London, 1826

COAL GAS

In the 1800s, many cities had a plant called a gasworks to produce "coal gas." Coal was brought to the gasworks and heated, and burnable gases were collected from the coal. The gas was piped through a city to light streetlamps. People used coal with a high gas content to make coal gas.

COAL FORMATION

MATTER	HOW IT FORMS	CARBON CONTENT
peat	dead plants accumulate without rotting completely	20%–25%
lignite	peat pressed and heated for millions of years	25%–35%
subbituminous coal	lignite pressed and heated for millions of years	35%–45%
bituminous coal	subbituminous coal pressed and heated for millions of years	45%–86%
anthracite	bituminous coal pressed and heated for millions of years	86%–97%

lignite

bituminous coal

anthracite **17**

WHERE IS COAL FOUND?

Coal is found all over the world wherever swamps and bogs existed millions of years ago. The largest coal deposits are traced back to certain time periods.

The prehistoric time from 360 to 300 million years ago is called the Carboniferous period. The many forests and swamps that existed during this time contained the plant life that led to large deposits of coal. Much bituminous coal of eastern North America and Europe is from this time. During the Permian period (300 to 250 million years ago), conditions were drier worldwide, and plant life changed to survive. Coal from this period can be found today in China, India, Russia, Australia, and Africa.

THE COAL GAP

There has been only one time when coal wasn't forming on Earth. At the end of the Permian period, more than 70 percent of land animal species and about 95 percent of oceanic species died out. Plant life was terribly affected as well, and coal stopped forming for several million years. Scientists call this the coal gap.

18

This is an artist's idea of a Carboniferous swamp that would later become a coal deposit. Because it takes so long for coal to form, it's called a nonrenewable resource. It can't be easily replaced.

19

HOW IS COAL MINED?

A bed of coal thick enough to be mined is a coal seam. Digging coal out of the seam is called mining. In ancient times, people dug tunnels into the ground to find coal. This is still one way to remove it. It's called underground, or deep, mining. Tunnels and chambers where coal is removed can lead hundreds of feet underground.

Today, if a coal seam is within 200 feet (61 m) of the surface, coal is removed through surface mining. Giant machines move away the rock and soil above the coal seam, and the coal is collected. Laws sometimes require that the rock and soil are then placed back where the coal used to be.

COAL AND INDUSTRY

As coal tunnels were dug deeper in England, flooding from underground water became a problem. Pumps were needed to remove the water. In 1765, James Watt invented a better coal-powered steam engine to power pumps. Watt's steam engine was later used in factories to power machines. This increased the demand for coal.

This is a surface mine with an exposed coal seam.

21

COAL POLLUTION

Mining for coal is a source of pollution. When coal is mined, rock and soil are removed and stored nearby. Rain can wash through the sediment and release pollutants into waterways. This practice can kill fish and plant life that live in the water. **Minerals** in upturned earth can contaminate, or pollute, water, too.

During surface mining, plants that grew above the coal seam are killed when they're uprooted by machines digging for coal. Though the replaced earth is often reseeded, it can take a long time for plant life to return. Sometimes, the soil isn't healthy enough to grow much new life.

COAL MINE DANGER

Coal mines can continue to produce acid **runoff** and pollute water after they're abandoned. Hikers can fall into old mine shafts, and underground explorers can be buried if a mine caves in. Coal mines can even catch fire! It's believed that thousands of old coal mines are on fire around the world.

A coal mine is responsible for the acid runoff you can see in this photo.

23

Burning coal is another source of pollution. It produces carbon dioxide, and extra carbon dioxide contributes to **climate change**. Coal burning is the source of one-third of all extra carbon dioxide in the atmosphere.

The elements nitrogen and sulfur in coal smoke mix with water vapor in clouds and fall as "acid rain," harming crops, forests, soil, and waterways. Burning coal can also produce nitrogen oxides, air pollutants that contribute to smog, which is a mixture of fog, smoke, and pollutants. Smog can cause **respiratory** illnesses.

Coal contains small amounts of nearly every element, some of which are toxic. Burning it can release mercury and other dangerous metals.

LEFTOVER ASH

Ash is the part of coal that doesn't burn, including some minerals. Fly ash is carried up by smoke, but is mostly trapped by screens. Heavier ash is left behind. In 2012, about 800 million tons (725 million mt) of burned coal in the United States left about 110 million tons (100 million mt) of coal ash. While some coal ash can be reused, such as for bricks, ash that's too toxic is just trash.

This land is covered by ash left over from burning coal.

25

YOU DECIDE

Why is coal used to produce more than 40 percent of the world's electricity if it causes so many problems? It's currently the cheapest source of energy.

Electricity is also made using wind and sunlight, but these natural resources aren't always available. Other energy sources have drawbacks, too. Hydroelectric power, or water-generated electricity, can harm waterways. Nuclear power plants produce dangerous waste. Natural gas can be burned to make electricity cheaply, but still releases carbon dioxide.

Are you willing to pay more for cleaner energy? Are you willing to use less coal-powered electricity for a cleaner planet? You decide.

A BETTER WAY TO BURN

There's a coal burner that results in fewer pollutants called a fluidized bed boiler. Crushed coal is mixed with limestone. Air blows the mixture around. While the coal burns, the limestone absorbs, or takes in, sulfur so that it isn't released into the air. The coal also burns at a lower temperature, creating fewer nitrogen oxides.

sun

wind

geothermal

steam

turbine

generator

water reservoir

Another source of energy is heat from Earth's core. This is called geothermal energy. It's only accessible, or easy to get to, in certain areas, though.

THE FUTURE OF COAL?

In the United States, new sources of natural gas are being used to produce electricity. In 2015, electricity made from natural gas exceeded the amount of electricity made from coal for the first time. That isn't the trend for all countries, though.

India is planning to build more than 400 new coal plants. In Germany and other European countries, people are concerned about the dangers of nuclear power, so new coal power plants will replace nuclear plants in those places.

For now, coal—a natural resource millions of years in the making—remains an important source of energy around the world.

TONS OF COAL

Eighty percent of the world's coal is found in just 10 countries. They are: the United States, Russia, China, Australia, India, Germany, Ukraine, Kazakhstan, Colombia, and Canada. The United States alone has more than 260 billion tons (235 billion mt) of coal! China is currently the biggest producer and consumer.

Many US coal plants are expected to close in the future. Whether cleaner sources of energy will take their place is uncertain.

GLOSSARY

bog: an area with wet ground, mostly made up of plant matter that's breaking down

climate change: long-term change in Earth's climate, caused partly by human activities such as burning oil and natural gas

deposit: an amount of a mineral in the ground that built up over a period of time

depression: an area that is lower than the surface surrounding it

environment: the natural world in which a plant or animal lives

generator: a machine that uses moving parts to produce electrical energy

heat value: an amount of heat produced from the complete burning of an amount of fuel

mineral: matter in the ground that forms rocks

molecule: a very small piece of matter, consisting of one or more atoms

respiratory: relating to breathing or the body system that takes in and uses oxygen

runoff: water from rain or snow that flows over the surface of the ground into streams

volcano: an opening in a planet's surface through which hot, liquid rock sometimes flows

FOR MORE INFORMATION

BOOKS

Doeden, Matt. *Finding Out About Coal, Oil, and Natural Gas.* Minneapolis, MN: Lerner Publications Company, 2015.

Somervill, Barbara. *The Story Behind Coal.* Chicago, IL: Heineman Library, 2012.

Tabak, John. *Coal and Oil.* New York, NY: Facts on File, 2009.

WEBSITES

Coal Basics
www.eia.gov/Kids/energy.cfm?page=coal_home-basics
Learn about the formation of coal and its uses.

Coal Facts
www.sciencekids.co.nz/sciencefacts/chemistry/coal.html
Read these interesting coal facts.

INDEX